The economic landscape is marked by a stark contrast between the wealthy elite and the mainstream population.

While the majority strives for financial stability, a select few seem to effortlessly navigate the realms of affluence.

Understanding the factors that distinguish the wealthy from the mainstream is a complex endeavor, as it involves a combination of personal choices, opportunities, and societal structures.

This book delves into the multifaceted nature of wealth disparity, examining the various aspects that contribute to the divergence between the privileged few and the broader populace.

Financial Literacy and Education:

One key differentiator between the wealthy and the mainstream is their level of financial literacy and education.

The affluent often possess a deeper understanding of investment strategies, risk management, and wealth accumulation.

They are more likely to make informed decisions regarding their finances, taking advantage of opportunities that may elude the mainstream population.

Access to quality education and resources that promote financial literacy can significantly impact an individual's ability to accumulate and grow wealth.

Income Disparities:

The most evident factor separating the wealthy from the mainstream is the substantial disparity in income. The wealthy often have multiple income streams, including investments, business ownership, and passive income.

In contrast, the mainstream relies predominantly on earned income from employment. Policies that perpetuate income inequality and limit upward mobility contribute to the widening gap between the two groups.

Asset Accumulation:

 Wealthy individuals prioritize asset accumulation, diversifying their portfolios to include real estate, stocks, bonds, and other high-return investments. Mainstream individuals, on the other hand, may face barriers to entry in the investment world due to limited resources or lack of knowledge. Asset accumulation becomes a compounding factor, as the wealthy leverage their assets to generate additional income, perpetuating the cycle of wealth accumulation.

Networking and Social Capital:

The ability to establish and maintain valuable connections is a distinguishing factor between the wealthy and the mainstream.

Networking provides access to opportunities, partnerships, and insider information that can significantly impact financial success.

The affluent often belong to social circles that facilitate networking, while mainstream individuals may lack such connections.

This social capital extends beyond financial opportunities, influencing career advancements, business ventures, and access to exclusive resources.

Entrepreneurship and Risk-Taking:

Entrepreneurial endeavors and a willingness to take calculated risks are common traits among the wealthy. Starting and growing a business requires a certain level of risk tolerance and a willingness to invest time and resources without immediate returns.

Mainstream individuals may be more risk-averse due to financial constraints or fear of failure, limiting their potential for wealth creation through entrepreneurial ventures.

Inheritance and Generational Wealth:

The transfer of wealth from one generation to the next plays a significant role in perpetuating economic disparities. Wealthy families often pass down assets, businesses, and financial knowledge to their descendants, creating a cycle of generational wealth.

Mainstream individuals may lack the inheritance and support systems that enable the wealthy to start their financial journey from a position of advantage.

Access to Opportunities:

 Access to opportunities, whether in education, employment, or business, is a critical factor influencing financial success. Wealthy individuals often have access to exclusive opportunities that may not be readily available to the mainstream.

 This includes elite educational institutions, high-profile job placements, and business partnerships that can propel them into higher income brackets.

Tax Structures and Financial Planning:

Wealthy individuals often engage in sophisticated tax planning to minimize their tax liabilities, utilizing legal loopholes and strategic financial structures.

Mainstream individuals, lacking the resources or knowledge for such endeavors, may find themselves subject to higher tax rates, limiting their ability to accumulate wealth.

Disparities in tax structures contribute to the widening gap between the wealthy and the mainstream.

The factors that separate the wealthy from the mainstream are intricate and interconnected.

Income disparities, financial literacy, networking, and generational wealth all contribute to the perpetuation of economic inequality.

Addressing these issues requires a multifaceted approach that encompasses education reform, inclusive economic policies, and initiatives to level the playing field.

Understanding the nuances of wealth disparity is crucial for creating a more equitable society where opportunities for financial success are accessible to a broader spectrum of individuals.

The following pages are left for your notes: